Contents

Introduction

What a glorious season Christmas is—because we have a glorious Savior! My deepest desire for you this Christmas is that the Lord Jesus will become more precious and near to you than He has ever been before. My prayer is that this little book might become a beautiful part of your Christmas this year in one of three ways.

A Christmas Gift. First, if you give or receive this as a gift on Christmas Day, turn to the December 25th selection and share the Special Christmas Celebration with your family on Christmas Day! Then read the daily selections as a family for the rest of the year. What a wonderful way to celebrate the Savior's birth and bring in the new year with the Savior's blessing!

A Christmas Preparation. Better yet, if you receive your copy before December first, make the twenty-four days preceding Christmas wonderful days of preparation, with Christmas a day of special celebration, and the rest of the year a heart-felt time of reflection.

A Family Tradition. Best of all, keep this little book as a family Christmas treasury—to reread, reflect upon and reaffirm the glorious gift of our gracious Savior year after year.

However this book comes into your home, may the devotional reflections in these pages draw you closer to the One who is God's perfect Gift—to Jesus Himself, our steadfast *love*, our shining *light*, our saving *lamb*, our sovereign *Lord*, and our satisfying *life*.

Lastly, note that each day's devotional includes an activity to help you apply these truths to your life and your family. Some are especially suitable for young children or grandchildren, some especially for families with older children. So above all, feel free to pick and choose the ones that are best for your own family—and don't be afraid to create your own family memories!

God bless you and keep you, and may the Christ of Christmas reveal Himself to you in a new and dynamic way!

Adrian Rogers

Jesus the
Steadfast Love

For God so loved the world that He gave His only begotten Son, that whoever believes in Him should not perish but have everlasting life.

J O H N   3 : 1 6

Though I speak with the tongues of men and angels, but have not love, I have become as sounding brass or a clanging cymbal.

1   C O R I N T H I A N S   1 3 : 1

Love Came Down

id you know that the true message of Christmas is found in John 3:16? Jesus said, "For God so loved the world that He gave His only begotten Son, that whoever believes in Him should not perish but have everlasting life."

This is the heart of Christmas. Jesus is God's great love gift, because Jesus came to give His life that we might have life and "have it to the full" (John 10:10). Without a doubt, *love came down at Christmas*.

Now because Jesus loved us enough to die on the cross for our sins, what better Christmas gift could we give others than to share His love with them, that they might have life? Love is a gift our world desperately needs this Christmas season.

In order to know and share Christ's love, we need to know how Christlike love looks and acts. And the best place to find a well-rounded description of love is in the Bible's great love chapter, 1 Corinthians 13.

Let's concentrate on verse 1. What Paul has in mind here is the *agapé* love of God. In verse 1, Paul writes, "Though I speak with the tongues of men and of angels, but have not love, I have become as sounding brass or a clanging cymbal." What Paul is saying here is that love is absolutely indispensable. The finest oratory on earth is no substitute for love.

We've all heard the expression, "He talks a better game than he plays." Paul isn't forbidding us to talk about love. We need to be a witness. But when it comes to sharing Christ's love this Christmas, we need to back up our verbal witness with the quality of our lives!

A C T I V I T Y

Provide family members with a blank Christmas card so that they can write their own Christmas message to someone they love outside your immediate family circle. Help younger children write their message, and allow them to color or decorate their card.

And though I have the gift of prophecy, and
understand all mysteries and all knowledge, and
though I have all faith, so that I could remove
mountains, but have not love, I am nothing.
And though I bestow all my goods to feed the
poor, and though I give my body to be burned,
but have not love, it profits me nothing.

1 CORINTHIANS 13:2–3

The Value of Love

ow important is love? Think of its value. According to 1 Corinthians 13:2-3, it's more important than a lot of things we consider to be important. In verse 2, Paul gives us a very impressive list of gifts and abilities that, taken together, add up to nothing when Christlike love is missing from our lives.

The gift of prophecy is the first gift on Paul's list (v. 2). I know enough about preaching to know that if you want to get a crowd, you can announce that you are going to preach a series of messages on prophecy. Man has an insatiable curiousity about prophecy. Far more people will come to hear a Bible study on prophecy than on love. But Paul says that love is greater than prophecy.

And then Paul says love is greater than knowledge. People today value knowledge tremendously. They almost worship it. But as John Wesley, the founder of Methodism, once said, "All knowledge without love is splendid ignorance."

According to 1 Corinthians 13:2, love is even greater than faith. Now faith is incredibly important. You cannot know God without faith. Paul even strengthens the contrast here by talking about mountain-moving faith. What believer would not long for mountain-moving faith? Yet without love, even this mountain-moving kind of faith is nothing. What good is it to remove mountains if you can't remove malice from your heart?

Are you giving people the gift of love this Christmas? Verse 3 of 1 Corinthians 13 fits right in this theme, because it talks about feeding the poor and even giving our lives for the sake of others.

Surely there is nothing greater you can do than to give all you have or lay down your life for another.

Some people give money instead of love. You can give without loving, but you cannot love without giving. People need to see Christmas love in action. How will you show Christ's love this Christmas?

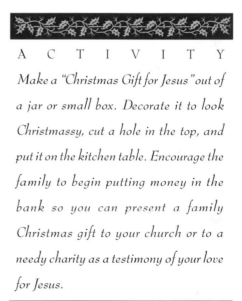

A   C   T   I   V   I   T   Y

Make a "Christmas Gift for Jesus" out of a jar or small box. Decorate it to look Christmassy, cut a hole in the top, and put it on the kitchen table. Encourage the family to begin putting money in the bank so you can present a family Christmas gift to your church or to a needy charity as a testimony of your love for Jesus.

Love suffers long and is kind;

love does not envy;

love does not parade itself,

is not puffed up.

1 CORINTHIANS 13:4

The Virtues of Love

We come now to a marvelous section of verses in 1 Corinthians 13:4–13 that gives us the characteristics of true, Christlike love. Today we want to look at the virtues of love mentioned in verse 4.

I think you'll agree with me that we are going to need to display these virtues during the Christmas season. Even with all the joy and delight of this special season, Christmas can also be a time of high stress for many individuals and families.

We need patience, with ourselves and others. So the first virtue of love Paul mentions in verse 4 is that love "suffers long." That is,

love is literally "long of temper." It is patient. It doesn't fly off the handle at the slightest provocation.

Some people say, "Well, I don't have much patience." What they are really saying is, "I don't have much love." A lack of patience is in reality a lack of love.

Then we read that love "is kind." Christmas is a season when even people who aren't ordinarily kind try to make an effort to be nice to others. But for the child of God, being kind is not a one-time effort. Kindness and courtesy are to characterize our treatment of people every day. Don't ever underestimate what kindness can do. The world is watching to see if we care.

Third, real love "does not envy." In other words, it is not jealous. If you have love, you'll be willing to give credit where credit is due. You're not going to think that somebody else's gain is your loss. You won't cringe when other people are recognized.

A fourth virtue of true love is humility. How our world needs a large dose of this! We're so used to people bragging and swaggering. But love doesn't "puff up" the heart with pride and cause the head to swell with self-importance. True love says, "I am sorry. I was wrong. Please forgive me."

If you and your family radiate these virtues of love, this will truly be a merry Christmas for you!

A C T I V I T Y

Using the four virtues of love listed in the verse for today, compose a family poem or a song that expresses your desire to show the love of Christ to each other and to the world this Christmas.

Jesus the Steadfast Love

Love . . . does not behave rudely, does not seek its

own, is not provoked, thinks no evil; does not

rejoice in iniquity, but rejoices in the truth;

bears all things, believes all things,

hopes all things, endures all things.

1 CORINTHIANS 13:5 – 7

Love Is Not Rude Nor Selfish

ontinue to think with me about additional virtues of love. How many times have you heard someone say, "Well, I just say what I think. I tell it like it is"?

More often than not, "telling it like it is" is an excuse for rudeness. It springs from a lack of love. According to Paul, love "does not behave itself rudely" (v. 5). He is referring to unseemly, ill-mannered behavior. Love is not that way!

Good manners can be a tremendous witness for Christ at Christmas. When the lines at the store get long and tempers get short, a word spoken in well-mannered love can soothe the troubled waters.

The apostle Paul follows this with another crucial quality of Christlike love: Love "does not seek its own." Another way to say this is that love is not selfish. Our problem as sinful human beings is that we want what we want when we want it. If we would cure selfishness, it would be like replanting the Garden of Eden!

Christmas is a wonderful time for a lesson on selflessness, especially with children. Little eyes and hearts often become filled with unbridled desire as children begin thinking about the gifts they want for Christmas.

We all need to remember a truth that Jesus taught: "It is more blessed to give than to receive" (Acts 20:35).

Real love is also even-tempered, or "not easily provoked." It doesn't have a hair trigger. Neither is love suspicious. It "thinks no evil." What that means is, love doesn't think the worst. It's not paranoid. It doesn't join the society of mudslingers. The person who doesn't trust anyone does not really know true love.

In verse 6, Paul mentions another virtue of love. He says that love does not take satisfaction in sin. It's one thing to sin, but it's another to rejoice in sin or to brag about it. Love rejoices when truth triumphs, not when evil does.

Finally, love "bears all things, believes all things, hopes all things, [and] endures all things" (v. 7). That doesn't mean we should love and endorse wickedness. But it does mean that we will love those who have failed, just as God has loved us.

ACTIVITY

Have each family member make a Christmas gift list. Collect the lists and then pray over each item. Ask God to show you whether He would be pleased for you to give this gift. Close by praying that He will help your family give more than it receives. Indeed, "It is more blessed to give than to receive."

Love never fails. But whether there are prophecies,
they will fail; whether there are tongues, they will
cease; whether there is knowledge, it will vanish
away. For we know in part and we prophesy in
part. But when that which is perfect has come,
then that which is in part will be done away.

1 CORINTHIANS 13:8–10

The Victory of Love

 et's consider the victory of love found in the wonderful declaration of verse 8: "Love never fails."

That's one of the greatest statements in the Bible. Love is eternal. It will never pass away.

Notice the things that will pass away, however. Prophecy, tongues, and knowledge are impressive gifts, but they will all pass away. Remember verse 2, where Paul says that prophecy, knowledge, and faith add up to nothing without love.

Paul is telling us not to get puffed up about what we know, because when it's all said and done we only know "in part" (v. 9).

The truth is that we don't know one percent of anything. Some people think they know the future, but all they really have is an educated guess, or maybe a hunch.

We are also warned against getting puffed up about the gifts we possess. The gift of tongues was one of the more spectacular spiritual gifts for the early church, but the gift of tongues fades and will be stilled. Love, however, endures.

A little child can ask questions about heaven that a doctor of theology can't answer. We need humility in these areas. But one thing we *can* know is that love will last. Love is more important than education. It's more important than ability. It is more important than prophecy. All of these things are going to pass away.

May your family be known for the Gospel it shares and the love it shows. Wouldn't it be wonderful to be famous for the Gospel and famous for love? When Christmas guests walk into your home, may they say, "This is a home that loves."

Love is not only the greatest virtue; it is also the greatest commandment. Jesus Himself said that love for God is the first and greatest commandment (Matt. 22:37–40).

If love is the greatest commandment, then what would be the greatest sin? It must be the failure to love, because that would be breaking the greatest commandment. Love is the greatest virtue and the greatest commandment. It is the greatest testimony!

A C T I V I T Y

Read Matthew 22:37–40 and discuss together what it means to love the Lord Jesus with all of your heart, soul, and mind. Then ask this question: "In what ways do we love ourselves?" Remember that these are the ways we should show love for others.

For now we see in a mirror, dimly, but then face to

face. Now I know in part, but then I shall

know just as I also am known. And

now abide faith, hope, love, these

three, but the greatest of

these is love.

1 CORINTHIANS 13:12–13

The Greatest of These Is Love

There was once an aged Christian man who was dying. A friend came to see him, and the dying man said, "I've just had three other visitors. Two of them are gone, but the third visitor will stay with me forever."

The friend asked, "Who were these visitors?"

The aged man said, "Well, the first visitor was Faith. I visited with Faith and enjoyed Faith, but then I told Faith good-bye. I said, 'Thank God for your company, Faith. I have walked with you since I first trusted Christ. But now I'm going to die and I won't need you anymore, because Faith will be lost in sight when I get to heaven and see Jesus face to face.'"

Then he continued, "My second visitor was Hope. We also had a wonderful time. But then I said to Hope, 'Farewell, Hope. You've helped me in the hour of battle. You've been with me in distress when my heart was broken and when I've had so many needs. You've been there like a rock, like an anchor. But, Hope, I won't need you anymore. I'm going to heaven where hope turns to reality.'"

But then the man said, "The third visitor who came to see me is still with me, and will always be with me. His name is Love. I said to him, 'Love, you've been my friend. You've linked me to God. You've linked me to my fellowman. You have comforted and gladdened me in all of my pilgrimages.

"'Now I'm going to heaven. But, Love, I'm not going to leave you behind. You will enter the city of God with me. And you, my friend, will be perfected in heaven.'"

Is that not what the Bible says? Look at the final verses of 1 Corinthians 13. Of the three gifts Paul mentions, the greatest is love. Do you want to give others the best Christmas gift possible? Give them the love of Christ. He is our life, our joy. He is the story of Christmas.

A   C   T   I   V   I   T   Y

Have each family member answer this question: "If you could have only one gift this Christmas, what would it be and why?" Let everyone share and then close by thanking God for His great love gift of the Lord Jesus.

Jesus the
Shining Light

The people who walked in darkness

Have seen a great light;

Those who dwelt in the land of the shadow of death,

Upon them a light has shined.

ISAIAH 9:2

A Great Light

f there is one truth that leaps out at us from the pages of Scripture at Christmas, it is that Jesus came to be the Light of the world! Light came into this dark world when Jesus was born in Bethlehem.

The prophet Isaiah calls Jesus "a great light" who has shined on those who "walked in darkness" (Isa. 9:2). The prophet is referring to spiritual darkness, which also is very great. But the darkness was no match for the light of God's Messiah, the Lord Jesus Christ.

Zechariah, the father of John the Baptist, also anticipated the coming of the Savior. In his great song of praise, he prophesied that Jesus would "give light to those who sit in darkness and the shadow of death, to guide our feet into the way of peace" (Luke 1:79).

Another man of God by the name of Simeon pointed to the Light. As Joseph and Mary came to the temple to dedicate the infant Jesus, Simeon took the baby to bless Him. God revealed to Simeon the identity of the Child, and he rejoiced that God had sent "a light to bring revelation to the Gentiles, and the glory of your people Israel" (Luke 2:32).

No matter where you turn in God's Word, you will find that Christmas is about light! We love to sing the Christmas carol, "Silent Night, Holy Night." But this great hymn is not about the night or about darkness. It's about the Light. The third stanza of "Silent Night" says, "Son of God, / love's pure light / Radiant beams from Thy holy face, / With the dawn of redeeming grace."

We sing another Christmas carol, "Hark! The Herald Angels Sing." The last stanza invites us to "Hail the heaven-born Prince of Peace! / Hail the Son of righteousness! / Light and life to all He brings, / Risen with healing in His wings."

We sing at Christmas because we have something to sing about! Light has come into the world, and we don't ever need to walk in darkness again!

A   C   T   I   V   I   T   Y

Give each family member an unlit candle (or a flashlight for younger children). Light your candle and then turn out the lights. Begin reading John 1:1–9. Each time you read the word light, *stop and use your candle to light another (or have the small children turn on their flashlights) until everyone's candle is lit. Finish reading the text, then pray, thanking God for sending Jesus to be our light at Christmas.*

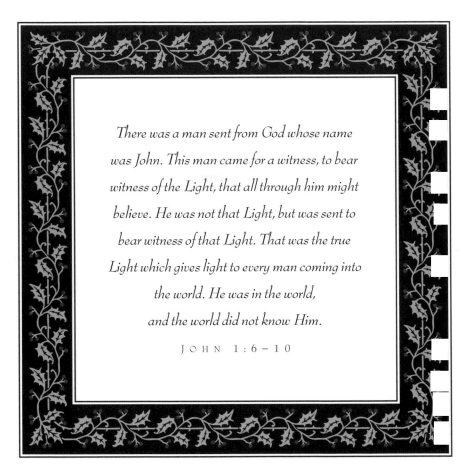

There was a man sent from God whose name was John. This man came for a witness, to bear witness of the Light, that all through him might believe. He was not that Light, but was sent to bear witness of that Light. That was the true Light which gives light to every man coming into the world. He was in the world, and the world did not know Him.

JOHN 1:6–10

The Purity of the Light

oday we want to emphasize Jesus as the purity of the light of Christmas.

The Bible says that Jesus was "in the world" (John 1:10). But the Lord was most assuredly not *of* this world. He did not have His origin in the world. His birth in Bethlehem was not the beginning of His life, for He is the Lord of heaven.

Because Jesus was not of this world, He is the pure, incorruptible Light. In the natural world, there is nothing as pure as light. Light can never be defiled or corrupted, no matter what it passes through or what it falls on. Light can never be debased or sullied.

You can shine light through a dirty windowpane or a glass of muddy water, and all the light does is expose the dirt. The light is not touched by the dirt.

Even the purest water flowing from a clear mountain spring will become contaminated as it flows along. Even the purest-looking crystals of snow falling from heaven contain tiny particles of debris. And as that snow falls on the ground, it will become corrupted. But light can never be defiled.

Therefore, light is a wonderful picture of the Lord Jesus Christ.

Jesus exposed sin, but He was never contaminated by sin. Jesus could touch sinners, but sin never touched Him. He was totally undefiled. When the Bible calls

Jesus the "light of the world," it's a reminder of the sinless, stainless purity of the Son of God.

Jesus was the only Person who could look other people in the face and say, "Can any of you prove me guilty of sin?" (John 8:46). The Baby born in Bethlehem was "the true Light" (John 1:9), the pure light of heaven. Jesus was in the world but not of the world. This Christmas, as we behold Jesus, the Light of the world, think about His incorruptible purity.

A C T I V I T Y

Take a few pinches of dirt from a potted plant and put them in a glass of clear water. Swirl the dirt around and then shine a flashlight through the glass as you explain that the light is untouched by the dirt. Ask a family member to pray that the purity of Jesus' light will shine through you in the new year ahead.

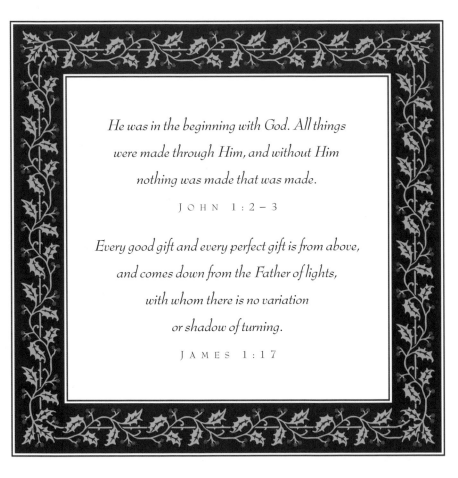

He was in the beginning with God. All things

were made through Him, and without Him

nothing was made that was made.

JOHN 1:2–3

Every good gift and every perfect gift is from above,

and comes down from the Father of lights,

with whom there is no variation

or shadow of turning.

JAMES 1:17

The Constancy of the Light

s we rejoice in the arrival of the Christmas season, let us celebrate the constancy of the light that shined into the world when Jesus was born of the virgin Mary.

John tells us that Jesus was "with God in the beginning" (John 1:2). Furthermore, Jesus is the Creator God without whom "nothing was made that has been made" (John 1:3). Jesus is the eternal God.

God cannot change. He declared through the prophet Malachi, "I am the LORD, I do not change" (Mal. 3:6). James made this wonderful statement: "Every good and perfect gift is from above, coming down from the Father of the heavenly lights, who does not change like shifting shadows" (James 1:17).

In the natural world, the speed of light is a constant. When Albert Einstein formulated his famous theory of relativity, he said he was able to put forward this theory because there is one thing and one thing alone in the world that is constant—the speed of light. Everything else is relative.

Light is the only thing that is constant in our natural universe. And Jesus is our one constant in the spiritual realm. Even the sun, which has never failed to give its light since the day God created it, will one day cease to shine.

We are told that the energy of the sun is slowly being used up. You won't have to worry about the sun burning out in our lifetime, but even the sun is not eternal. Its light will not shine endlessly. The light of Jesus, however, will illumine heaven throughout all eternity. What a wonderful truth to consider this Christmas!

We will soon welcome a new year. And though our world is a very uncertain place, we have this certainty to lean on: "His compassions fail not. They are new every morning; great is Your faithfulness" (Lam. 3:22–23).

Not only do we have the constancy of Jesus to depend on for today, but someday we are going to be made just like Him (1 John 3:2). We will bask in the direct rays of His glorious light forever! Praise God for the changeless, constant light of the Lord Jesus Christ!

A C T I V I T Y

Gather a stack of old magazines and ask each family member to find a picture of something that expresses his or her joy over the fact that Jesus never changes. Share your discoveries with each other, and close by singing the last stanza of "Silent Night."

In Him was life, and

the life was the light of men.

JOHN 1:4

And this is the testimony; that God has given us

eternal life, and this life is in His Son.

1 JOHN 5:11

The Vitality of the Light

 ohn 1:4 says of Jesus, "In Him was life, and that life was the light of men." Here is the vitality of the light.

Light and life are inextricably interwoven. You cannot have life without light. When God wanted to bring life out of chaos in creation, He said, "Let there be light" (Gen. 1:3). When the light appeared, the seas began to swarm with life. The seeds of earth began to bud and blossom.

I've always loved natural science. I can remember that the first big word I ever really locked in on was *photosynthesis*. I remember being enthralled as my teacher explained the meaning and process of photosynthesis.

She told us, "The word *photo* means 'light,' and the word *synthesis* means 'to put together.' Green plants produce food by putting chemicals together with light."

It is light that causes these plants to produce food, and the whole life chain of animals and humans depends on this process. Life itself is built on sunlight. Without sunlight, our world would become cold and dark and dead.

When Jesus was born in Bethlehem, He came to give us life. When the Holy Spirit shined the light of the Gospel into our hearts, a divine photosynthesis took place producing life where before there was only death. "The unfolding of your words gives light," says the psalmist (Ps. 119:130). Jesus is the Light.

Do you know that life followed Jesus everywhere He went during his earthly ministry? Jesus said, "I am come that they may have life, and that they may have it more abundantly" (John 10:10).

No matter how cold and dark your world may seem, it can be brought back to life when the glorious light of the Son of God shines into your heart.

There is no life without light. The life and the light went out of Adam's race when he sinned in the Garden of Eden. But when we come to Christ, the Lord comes back in, turns on the light, and life begins again.

Jesus is the Light of the world. That little Babe in Bethlehem turned on the light and gave us eternal life.

A C T I V I T Y

Go into an inner room in your home and make it as dark as possible. Then turn out the light, and after 30 seconds, light a single match. Talk about how light overcomes darkness and how Jesus has brought us eternal life, overcoming the darkness of sin.

Jesus the Shining Light

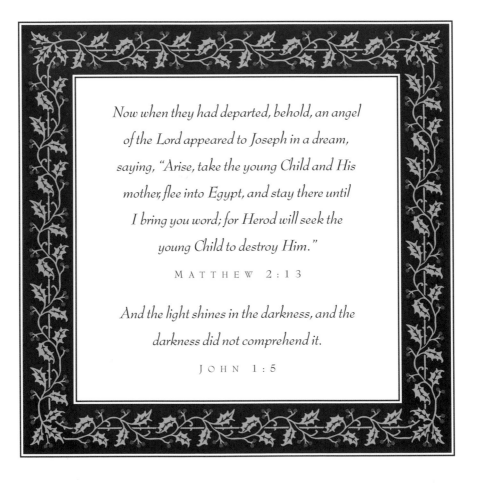

Now when they had departed, behold, an angel

of the Lord appeared to Joseph in a dream,

saying, "Arise, take the young Child and His

mother, flee into Egypt, and stay there until

I bring you word; for Herod will seek the

young Child to destroy Him."

MATTHEW 2:13

And the light shines in the darkness, and the

darkness did not comprehend it.

JOHN 1:5

The Victory of Light

Here is another truth about the light of Christmas that will bless you this Christmas season. It's found in John 1:5, where the apostle writes, "The light shines in the darkness, and the darkness did not comprehend it." I want to talk with you today about the victory of the light.

What does John mean when he says that the darkness could not "understand" or "comprehend" the light? This word has also been rendered "overcome," "put out," or "extinguish." What John is talking about is the victory of light over darkness.

All of history is really a battle between light and darkness. We see it even at the birth of Jesus in the account of King Herod's murderous rampage against the baby boys in Bethlehem. The darkness attempted to extinguish God's light.

But who must win this battle? As surely as day follows night, it is clear that darkness has no power against light! As the hymn says, "Jesus shall reign where'er the sun / Does his successive journeys run."

If you're in a dark room and you want to dispel the darkness, would you take the vacuum cleaner and vacuum the darkness out? Would you take a shovel and shovel it out? Of course not. All you have to do to conquer the darkness is turn on the light. When you do that, the darkness flees. It cannot stay. It is totally powerless against the light.

The energy produced by our sun is beyond what we can imagine. On the brightest moonlit night, the light of the moon is only one eight-hundred-thousandth as bright as the sunshine on an ordinary day. If you look directly into the sun, you will burn your eyes. Yet, for all of its incredible power, the sun is at best only a faint illustration of the Son of God in His brightness.

No one can overcome or extinguish the Lord's light! In Him there is victory, at Christmas and every other season of the year. Let's release the light of the Lord Jesus Christ into the world this Christmas. Let's bear witness to the Light!

A   C   T   I   V   I   T   Y

Imagine what it must have been like to be a shepherd in Bethlehem on the night Jesus was born, when the light of God burst through the darkness. Pretend you are one of those shepherds; write a letter to your mother describing what happened that night. Let each family member take part in telling the story.

Jesus the Shining Light

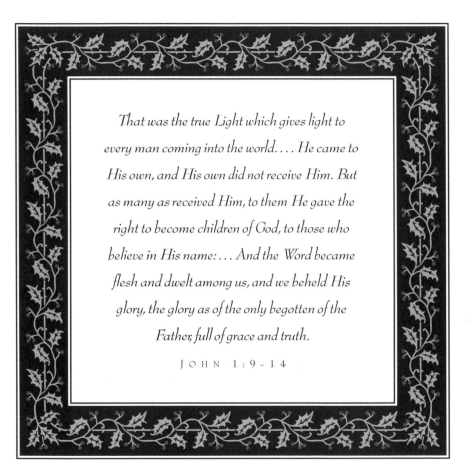

That was the true Light which gives light to every man coming into the world.... He came to His own, and His own did not receive Him. But as many as received Him, to them He gave the right to become children of God, to those who believe in His name:... And the Word became flesh and dwelt among us, and we beheld His glory, the glory as of the only begotten of the Father, full of grace and truth.

JOHN 1:9-14

The Glory of Light

et us consider the glory of the light who is our Savior and Lord, the Child of Bethlehem, Jesus Christ.

Again, the apostle John says of Jesus, "The Word became flesh and made his dwelling among us. We have seen his glory, the glory of the One and Only, who came from the Father, full of grace and truth" (John 1:14).

Do you know what glory is? It is the outshining of the light of Jesus' grace and truth. It's the *Shekinah,* the glory of God that filled first the tabernacle and then the temple of God in the Old

Testament. The glory is the light of God that is in Jesus Christ, who is Himself fully God.

I'm sure you know that light is made up of a spectrum of seven colors. The number seven reminds us of the perfections of God. When you put all seven of the colors of the spectrum together, the result is pure light, which speaks of the holiness of the Lord Jesus. Jesus is the One who makes everything colorful, everything glorious! He is the glory of God.

Let's think for a minute about those who refuse the Light. It's sad, but true, that many say *no* to the Light. John makes this clear in verses 10–11 of our text. Jesus came to that which was His own, but they refused Him.

A person would be foolish to deny the existence of light just because he can't see it. Some people can't see the light of Jesus because they don't want to see it. But we are called to take the light of Christmas to those who walk in the darkness.

And the good news is that if people without Christ will only look to Him, He will shine His light into their hearts! The Babe of Bethlehem is the Light of the world. He will dispel the darkness with the glory of His presence for anyone who will ask.

A   C   T   I   V   I   T   Y

Make a list of people you know who need Christ in their lives, and begin praying that God will open their hearts to Jesus. Keep your list with you throughout the Christmas season, and ask God to give your family an opportunity to share the Gospel with these people.

Jesus the Saving Lamb

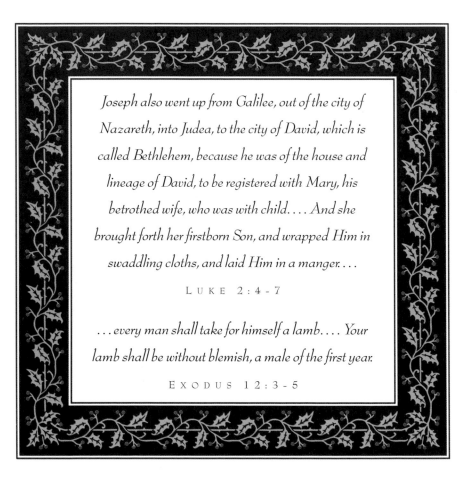

Joseph also went up from Galilee, out of the city of Nazareth, into Judea, to the city of David, which is called Bethlehem, because he was of the house and lineage of David, to be registered with Mary, his betrothed wife, who was with child.... And she brought forth her firstborn Son, and wrapped Him in swaddling cloths, and laid Him in a manger....

LUKE 2:4-7

...every man shall take for himself a lamb.... Your lamb shall be without blemish, a male of the first year.

EXODUS 12:3-5

The Prophecy of the Lamb

hen I was a little boy, I learned a nursery rhyme that went like this: "Mary had a little lamb, its fleece was white as snow." Well, Mary's Christmas Lamb was the virgin-born Son of God!

We read in Luke chapter 2 that when the Roman decree went out for a census of the Roman world, Mary and Joseph went to Bethlehem. Now we know that it was not incidental or accidental that Jesus was born in Bethlehem. That little village about five miles south of Jerusalem would probably have passed into obscurity except for that one wonderful night. The event that took place that first Christmas had been prophesied centuries earlier by the prophet Micah (5:2).

It was fitting that Mary's Lamb would be born in Bethlehem. Why? Because for centuries, the Jewish priests had been raising Passover lambs in Bethlehem! In those shepherds' fields outside Bethlehem, a very special breed of sacrificial lambs was raised and nurtured, that those lambs might be brought to Jerusalem.

At Passover, those lambs were sacrificed to cover the sins of the people. Mary's little Lamb came to be the final Passover lamb, the one sacrifice for sin forever. The destiny of the entire world is wrapped up in Mary's little Lamb.

Today I want you to see the prophecy of the lamb. That's why you found Exodus 12 listed in today's Scripture reading. This chapter has some crucial things to say about the Lamb of Christmas.

The Israelites were in slavery in Egypt, groaning under the cruel bondage of Pharaoh. They needed to be redeemed. God had a plan to redeem His people and set them free, a plan wrapped up in a little lamb (Exod. 12:1-3).

Notice the qualifications for this lamb: It had to be "without blemish, a male of the first year" (v. 5). This lamb had to be perfect. Why? Because it was going to die to redeem God's people. What a wonderful picture of the Lord Jesus, the Lamb of Bethlehem!

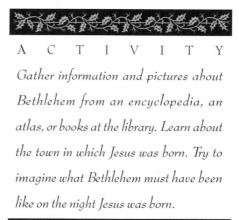

A   C   T   I   V   I   T   Y

Gather information and pictures about Bethlehem from an encyclopedia, an atlas, or books at the library. Learn about the town in which Jesus was born. Try to imagine what Bethlehem must have been like on the night Jesus was born.

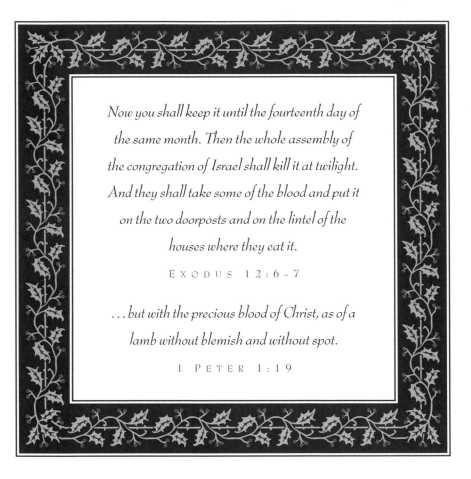

Now you shall keep it until the fourteenth day of the same month. Then the whole assembly of the congregation of Israel shall kill it at twilight. And they shall take some of the blood and put it on the two doorposts and on the lintel of the houses where they eat it.

EXODUS 12:6-7

...but with the precious blood of Christ, as of a lamb without blemish and without spot.

1 PETER 1:19

A Slain and Saving Lamb

e are considering the wonderful story of the birth of Mary's Lamb, the Lord Jesus Christ. At this Christmas season, we rejoice in God's gift of His sinless, spotless Lamb.

Today I want to take you back to the book of Exodus. Your celebration of Christmas will take on new meaning when you see that the Babe of Bethlehem was the Lamb of God.

Did you know that the symbol of ancient Egypt was a serpent? I once visited the British Museum in London and saw the crown that the Pharaohs would wear. There on that crown was a coiled serpent.

Here in the book of Exodus is a battle between a lamb and a serpent: a defenseless, gentle, meek and mild lamb, against a venomous, hissing, poisonous serpent.

The Passover lamb had to be a very special lamb (Exod. 12:5). One blemish would disqualify a lamb from being used for the Passover in Egypt. For generations after that night, Israel's priests would examine the Passover lambs very carefully, checking for the slightest flaw. Jesus, the Lamb of Bethlehem, was also "without blemish and without spot" (1 Peter 1:19).

But not only was Jesus a special lamb, He was a slain lamb (Exod. 12:5). On the appointed day, the father of the Israelite family was to slay the Passover lamb and catch its blood in a basin—another prophetic picture of Mary's little Lamb, who would be slain on a Roman cross.

This lamb was also a saving lamb. God told the Israelites to take the Passover lamb's blood and put it on the doorposts and the lintel of the house (v. 7). Whoever came into the house would be saved from death because they came in through and under the blood (Exod. 12:13). If you know the Christ of Christmas, you are safe under the blood!

A   C   T   I   V   I   T   Y

Send each family member through the house to bring back a variety of common household items you have put on a list (things such as kitchen utensils, dishes, books, cups, items of clothing). Point out that each item has some type of flaw and that nothing on earth is perfect. Then offer a prayer of thanks to God for Jesus, His perfect Lamb.

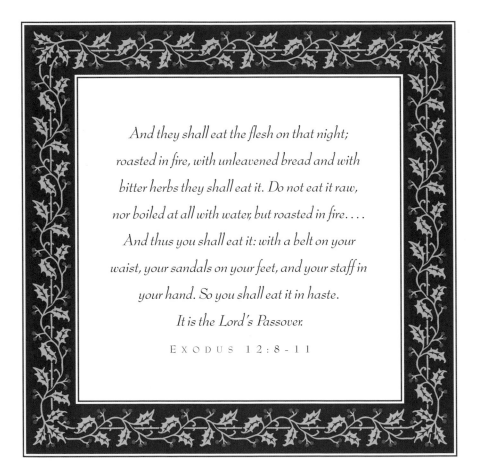

And they shall eat the flesh on that night;

roasted in fire, with unleavened bread and with

bitter herbs they shall eat it. Do not eat it raw,

nor boiled at all with water, but roasted in fire....

And thus you shall eat it: with a belt on your

waist, your sandals on your feet, and your staff in

your hand. So you shall eat it in haste.

It is the Lord's Passover.

EXODUS 12:8-11

A Shared Lamb

We're talking about Mary's little Lamb, Jesus, the One born in Bethlehem to "save his people from their sins" (Matt. 1:21). Today we will finish our look at the Lamb in prophecy.

Exodus 12:7 makes it clear that the only salvation for the Israelites in Egypt that first Passover night was to put the blood of the lamb on their doorposts. The Israelites could have encrusted their doors with jewels and gold, but that would have done no good. They could have tied an unblemished, living lamb outside their doors, but that would not have satisfied God's demand.

Salvation does not come from the life of Christ, but from the death of Christ. Salvation is not learning lessons from what Jesus did in life, but receiving life from what He did in His atoning death. The Bible says that without the shedding of blood there is no forgiveness of sin (Heb. 9:22).

This special Lamb, who was also a slain Lamb and a saving Lamb, then became a shared Lamb. Exodus 12:8 instructs the Israelites to roast and eat the lamb they had slain, along with unleavened bread and bitter herbs to remind them of the bitterness of their slavery.

But the key was the shedding of blood and sprinkling it on the entrance to the house. Verses 12-13 in Exodus chapter 12 spell out the judgment that was to fall that night. Praise God for the blood! "When I see the blood, I will pass over you, and the plague shall not be on you to destroy you when I strike the land of Egypt."

Can you imagine what it must have been like that night in Egypt? All the Egyptians smelled lamb roasting, because a quarter of a million or so households were preparing the Passover meal. As those Hebrews sat down to eat the lamb they had roasted, a bunch of slaves became a nation. When they walked out of Egypt, a lamb walked out inside of them!

A C T I V I T Y

Prepare a special meal in the next few days, using as many "family favorite" dishes as possible. As you serve each course, talk about the Passover meal and try to put yourselves in the place of a Hebrew family eating the lamb God had provided.

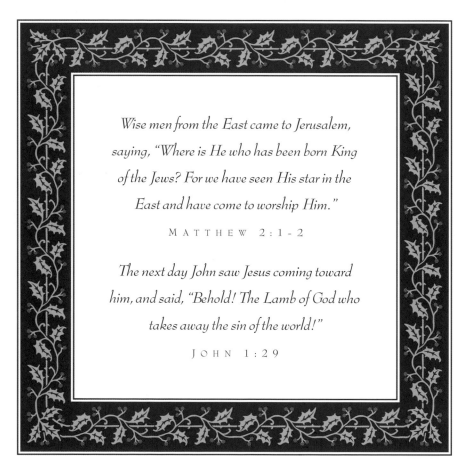

Wise men from the East came to Jerusalem,

saying, "Where is He who has been born King

of the Jews? For we have seen His star in the

East and have come to worship Him."

MATTHEW 2:1-2

The next day John saw Jesus coming toward

him, and said, "Behold! The Lamb of God who

takes away the sin of the world!"

JOHN 1:29

A Special Lamb in History

ary's little Lamb was the Christ of Christmas. We have seen the Lamb in prophecy.

Now let's consider the Lamb in history. The lamb of Exodus 12 only foreshadowed Mary's Lamb. But when Jesus was born in Bethlehem, the Lamb entered history. The wise men knew who He was. That's why they came to worship Mary's Lamb.

John the Baptist also knew that the One born on Christmas was a special Lamb. Years later, at the commencement of Jesus' public ministry, John saw Jesus coming and cried out, "Behold! The Lamb of God who takes away the sin of the world!" (John 1:29).

I want to say it again: Jesus was a special Lamb. He was the spotless, sinless, virgin-born Son of God. He was a miracle Lamb. Someone may say, "I believe the virgin birth is an impossibility." Well, I do too if you leave God out of it. But I also believe that with God all things are possible.

That little Baby wrapped in swaddling clothes, lying in Bethlehem's manger, was and is the eternal, uncreated, self-existing God—the great *I AM,* the Word made flesh. The Infinite became an infant. God lay in a manger.

We have seen from prophecy that Mary's little Lamb was a special Lamb and a slain Lamb. We see that in history too. John the Baptist declared that Jesus would take away the sin of the world. John was speaking of Jesus' atoning death on the cross.

This is why Jesus was born of a virgin. He had to be virgin-born in order to be sinless. Why was He sinless? So He could make a blood atonement. The Bible says it is the blood that makes atonement for sin.

A child's bloodline is established by the father, not by the mother. None of the baby's blood circulates through the mother's body. Mary was Jesus' earthly mother, but he had no earthly father. God was the Father of our Lord Jesus Christ, so the blood that flowed through the veins of Mary's Lamb was the very blood of God (Acts 20:28).

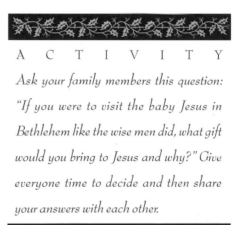

A C T I V I T Y

Ask your family members this question: "If you were to visit the baby Jesus in Bethlehem like the wise men did, what gift would you bring to Jesus and why?" Give everyone time to decide and then share your answers with each other.

Jesus the Saving Lamb

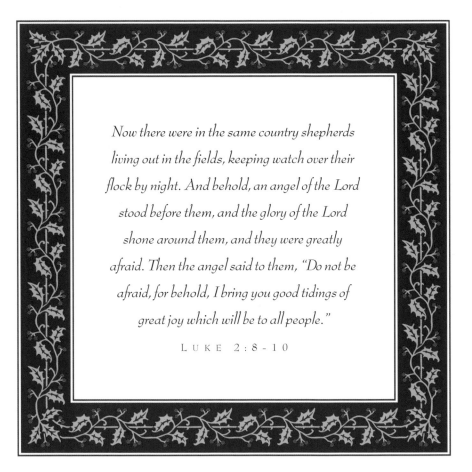

Now there were in the same country shepherds living out in the fields, keeping watch over their flock by night. And behold, an angel of the Lord stood before them, and the glory of the Lord shone around them, and they were greatly afraid. Then the angel said to them, "Do not be afraid, for behold, I bring you good tidings of great joy which will be to all people."

LUKE 2:8-10

A Perfect Lamb

What a wonderful Savior we have in Mary's Lamb, the Son of God born that first Christmas night!

Jesus came as He did, born of a virgin, to be what He was—the sinless Lamb of God. He was what He was, sinless, to do what He did—die for our sins. And He died for our sins so that He, being what He was, might make us what we are not and ought to be—children of God.

Remember those Passover lambs being raised in Bethlehem at the time of Jesus' birth? Those were the lambs the shepherds kept watching over when the angel appeared to them announcing the birth of the Savior.

Even though we are observing Christmas, the first week of Jesus' earthly life, I want to "fast forward" to the last week of His life. On Palm Sunday, the Lord Jesus came down the Mount of Olives and ascended to the temple mount. At the very same time, the lambs for the upcoming Passover were brought in through the sheep gate.

The priests examined those lambs to make certain they were perfect for sacrifice. At the same time, God's Lamb was examined by His enemies. No charge whatsoever could be made against Jesus. Even Pilate had to confess, "I find no fault in Him" (John 19:4). Jesus was a perfect Lamb.

Jesus went from the temple mount to the Last Supper and then out to dark Gethsemane. By nine o'clock the next morning, He was on His way to the cross.

Then at three o'clock that afternoon, as the priests offered the Passover lambs in the temple, Mary's Lamb was hanging on the cross. Suddenly He cried, "It is finished" (John 19:30). Our sin debt had been paid in full!

Have you been to Jesus for the cleansing power? Are you washed in the blood of the Lamb?

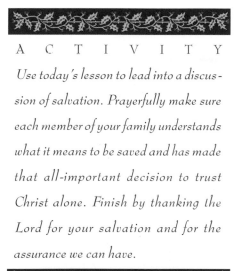

A C T I V I T Y

Use today's lesson to lead into a discussion of salvation. Prayerfully make sure each member of your family understands what it means to be saved and has made that all-important decision to trust Christ alone. Finish by thanking the Lord for your salvation and for the assurance we can have.

...in the midst of the throne...stood a Lamb as

though it had been slain, ... Then I looked, and

I heard the voice of many angels around the

throne, the living creatures, and the elders; and

the number of them was ten thousand times ten

thousand, and thousands of thousands, saying

with a loud voice:

"Worthy is the Lamb who was slain

To receive power and riches and wisdom,

And strength and honor and glory and blessing!"

REVELATION 5:6, 11−12

The Lamb in Victory and Majesty

here are two more glimpses of Mary's little Lamb I want to show you. The first one is the Lamb in victory.

In Revelation chapter 5, the apostle John had a glimpse into glory. He saw the throne of God, and then he noticed, in the right hand of the One sitting on the throne, a book sealed with seven seals.

This seven-sealed book is the title deed to the earth, the heavens, and the netherworld. It represents the right to rule. John saw that there was no one who could break the seals and open the book, and because of this he began to weep. One of the elders, however, said to him, "John, don't weep. Behold , the Lion of the tribe of Judah has prevailed to open the scroll and to loose its seven seals."

Now when John looked, he saw not a lion but a lamb (v. 6). The word used here for *lamb* is a special word, for it literally means "little lamb," that is, a pet lamb. This is Mary's little Lamb. What an amazing picture of the glorified Jesus!

John also saw a slain Lamb (v. 6), bearing the marks of the nails with which He was crucified. He will bear these marks forever. When we go to heaven, we will see those nail prints in His hands.

Jesus is not only a small Lamb and a slain Lamb, He is also a standing Lamb (v. 6). He laid down in death in a grave, but the grave could not hold Him. He stood up in resurrection, and He is standing in heaven today, making intercession for us.

This Lamb is also strong. He has "seven horns." In the Bible, horns are emblematic of power. This Lamb is omnipotent. He is also a searching Lamb, having "seven eyes" that speak of omniscience.

And then Jesus is the sovereign Lamb. Verse 7 says that He came and took the book out of the right hand of Him who sat on the throne. He alone is worthy to open it. This is the Lamb in victory.

The second glimpse I want to show you is of the Lamb in majesty (vv. 8–14). The song of the glorious heavenly beings is offered to Mary's little Lamb. Join me this Christmas season in saying with the heavenly hosts, "Worthy is the Lamb—exclusively, exceedingly, eternally worthy!"

A C T I V I T Y

Spend a few minutes worshiping the Lamb of God. Sing quietly together the final line of the Christmas carol "O Come, All Ye Faithful," adding these words, "For He alone is worthy, Christ the Lord."

Jesus the Saving Lamb

Jesus the Sovereign Lord

For there is born to you this day in the city of

David, a Savior, who is Christ the Lord.

LUKE 2:11

Jesus Is Savior and Lord

he Lordship of Jesus Christ is of paramount importance to you and your loved ones.

No matter where you turn in the New Testament, you are confronted with the indisputable fact that Jesus is Lord. If I had only one statement I could make to the world at this Christmas season, only one sentence I could utter, it would be the confession: "Jesus is Lord."

Look how we are confronted with Jesus' Lordship at the first Christmas. The angel announced to the shepherds that the One born in Bethlehem was the Savior, "who is Christ the Lord" (Luke 2:11). We see two things in this glorious verse.

First, we see the Christmas provision. This provision is a Savior. It has been well said that if our greatest need had been information, our Creator would have sent an educator. If our greatest need had been technology, God would have sent a scientist. If our greatest need had been money, we would have been given an economist.

But as our greatest needs were salvation and forgiveness, God sent a Savior! That's the Christmas provision.

Notice also the Christmas profession, which is the profession that "Jesus Christ is Lord." Now I dare say that many people say they believe in Christ's Lordship. But not everyone who says they believe Jesus is Lord is *living* in the light of that truth. The question is whether or not we have crowned Him Lord.

Is Jesus Lord of all you are, all you have, and all you do? Is He the Lord of your tongue? Is He the Lord of your thoughts? Is He the Lord of your time? Is He the Lord of your temper? Is He the Lord of your treasure?

The angel's declaration on that Christmas night is one we all have to recognize and deal with. The Christ of Christmas is Lord of all creation and Lord of His people!

A C T I V I T Y

Answer this question: If people were to do an in-depth investigation of your family's Christmas celebration this year, what evidence would they find that you have crowned Jesus as Lord of your home?

Therefore let all the house of Israel know

assuredly that God has made this Jesus, whom

you crucified, both Lord and Christ.

ACTS 2:36

Confessing Jesus as Lord

ave you crowned Jesus as Lord in your personal and family life?

Are you gladly, freely, and openly confessing Him as Lord? In Luke 2:10 the angel said that the announcement of Jesus' birth was "good tidings of great joy which will be to all people." God wants this message known around the world.

You see, the Lordship of Jesus is what separates the crowds at Christmas. Anybody can get sentimental about a little baby lying in a manger. Now make no mistake—I thank God for the "sweet little Jesus boy." The Bible's emphasis, however, is not on Jesus the infant, but on Jesus the Lord. Many of the same worldly people

Jesus the Sovereign Lord

who stand around the manger this week singing Christmas carols will be drunkenly singing "Auld Lang Syne" in a few days at New Year's Eve parties. They do not confess Jesus as Lord.

In Bible times, to openly and boldly confess "Jesus is Lord" really meant something. For a Jew to say that Jesus was Lord meant that He was Jehovah God, the eternal, self-existing God of the Old Testament.

The Jews held God's name in such reverence that they would not even pronounce it. The scribes copying the Scriptures would pick up a new pen to write the word *Lord*. For a Jew to confess Jesus as Lord meant paying a price—being excluded from the nation of Israel. But this was the truth that Peter declared to Israel in his great message at Pentecost in Acts chapter 2. He said, "Let all the house of Israel know assuredly that God has made this Jesus … both Lord and Christ."

Gentiles also had to pay a price for that confession, because it was deemed treason against Caesar to confess anyone else as Lord. It cost many early Christians persecution, and oftentimes death, to confess Jesus as Lord and Christ.

I wonder at this Christmas season, is Jesus your Lord in this way? Do you see Him as God? Do you confess Him as Lord no matter what the cost may be?

Jesus does not want prominence in your life; He deserves and demands preeminence. He is Lord!

A C T I V I T Y

Consider this question as a family: What would you be willing to give up in order to maintain your confession of Jesus as Lord?

… That if you confess with your mouth the
Lord Jesus and believe in your heart that God
has raised Him from the dead, you will be saved.
For with the heart one believes unto righteousness,
and with the mouth confession is
made unto salvation.

ROMANS 10:9–10

Sealing Salvation

I want to take the next four days to show you some of the wonderful things believing and confessing Jesus as Lord will do for you. We might call them Christmas presents that you will never have to exchange or return!

The first thing that believing and confessing Christ will do is seal your salvation. That's what Paul is talking about in Romans 10:9–10. He writes, "If you confess with your mouth the Lord Jesus and believe in your heart that God has raised Him from the dead, you will be saved. For with the heart one believes unto righteousness, and with the mouth confession is made unto salvation."

It's very clear. If Jesus is not your Lord, He's not your Savior. Today we hear people say, "You've accepted Christ as your Savior. Why not make Him Lord of your life?" But let me say it again. If Jesus Christ is not your Lord, He is not your Savior. Christ is not divided. Dr. Vance Havner used to say that salvation is not a cafeteria line where we order "a little Saviorhood today, but no Lordship, thank you."

The Christmas message is so plain. The word from heaven was clear. The Baby of Bethlehem was and is the Lord of the universe. The wise men who came so far to bow before Jesus and present their gifts acknowledged Him as the Sovereign Lord. The angels rejoiced at the glad announcement that the Messiah had been born.

Even the thief on the cross who was crucified next to Jesus confessed His Lordship and pleaded for salvation when he cried, "Lord, remember me when You come into Your kingdom" (Luke 23:42).

Jesus instantly accepted his confession, telling him, "Today you will be with Me in Paradise" (v. 43).

The good news of Christmas is that when you call on Jesus and say, "Lord, save me," He says to you, "Today it is done." Salvation is by grace through faith, and it is immediate and total. But you must be committed to Jesus' Lordship if you want His salvation.

A C T I V I T Y

Christ has given us Himself this Christmas. There is a gift we can give Him that He wants very much: our hearts! Have family members write a short poem or song or draw a picture that expresses their desire to give God their hearts this Christmas.

And they overcame him by the blood of the

Lamb and by the word of their testimony, and

they did not love their lives to the death.

REVELATION 12:11

Silencing Satan and Strengthening Saints

 onfessing Christ not only seals salvation, as we saw yesterday, but it also silences Satan. How Satan hopes that you and I will not learn to believe and confess that Christ is Lord. In Revelation 12:11, John writes that one way the saints overcame Satan was "by the word of their testimony."

What is this testimony? "Jesus is Lord." Satan is not afraid of you and me, but he is terrified by our testimony! Satan is conquered by confession.

When you take the name of Jesus Christ and boldly fling it in the face of Satan, he cowers. I have seen firsthand the power of the name of Jesus and the power of the confession that Jesus is Lord.

This is why Satan tried to destroy the infant Jesus through the evil King Herod. The devil knew full well who that Baby in Bethlehem was. Satan tried to kill Jesus because he knew that the manger of Bethlehem held his defeat.

Confessing Jesus as Lord not only seals salvation and silences Satan, it also strengthens saints. Do you want to be a strong Christian? Begin to confess openly and gladly that Jesus Christ is Lord— that He is *your* Lord!

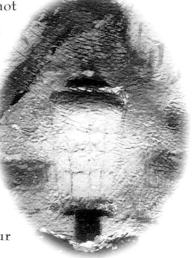

If you want your faith to be strong, put your faith in your

mouth. Begin to articulate it. You'll find that it will begin to grow. The more you assert something, the stronger its power will become in your own life. Confessing Jesus will increase your love for Him!

In Acts 10:14, Peter said, "Not so, Lord," in response to a command from heaven to eat "unclean" animals. Explain to your family that these two statements cannot go together. If Jesus is Lord, we must obey immediately, and we cannot say no to what He commands.

Now have everyone write this phrase from Acts 10:14 on a piece of paper and explain that we have to cross out either "Not so" or "Lord." Pray that God will give each of you the strength to obey Christ this Christmas and then have each person cross out the phrase that does not represent his or her commitment.

Jesus the Sovereign Lord

So they said, "Believe on the Lord Jesus Christ,

and you will be saved, you and your household."

A C T S   1 6 : 3 1

Saving Sinners

onfessing the Christ of Christmas as Lord also saves sinners.

Acts 16:31 is one of the most powerful and crystal-clear verses in all the New Testament. The jailer at Philippi didn't want a theological treatise. He was trembling. It was the middle of the night. His life was on the line. All he wanted to know was how to be saved. Paul cut through all the jargon to give him the essence of the Gospel. "Believe on the Lord Jesus Christ, and you will be saved."

We can't all be preachers like Paul, but we can all be reachers. We can all be testifiers. As we are rubbing elbows with so many

Jesus the Sovereign Lord

people this Christmas season, wouldn't it be wonderful if every believer would share the "good tidings of great joy" with at least one other person?

When believers are bold in their witness for Christ, history can be changed. The apostle Paul is the best example of that. He not only shook things up in Philippi, but he and his fellow servants also turned the whole Roman world on its head.

Do you remember the revolution in the country of Romania when the Iron Curtain of communism fell? As the truth came out, we learned that what happened in Romania was not really a political revolution. It was a spiritual revival.

It started with a pastor who had been told he couldn't freely preach the message of Jesus. One day this pastor got on his knees, and God told him to be bold. He called a few other believers around him, and they agreed that whether they lived or died, they were going to stand for God.

The Communist soldiers came to this pastor's house to arrest him. But he stood there, unflinching, and his church members came and stood between the soldiers and their pastor. Then more and more people came, until there were thousands shouting, "There is a God! There is a God!" And a brutal Communist regime eventually fell.

Let's not be intimidated into silence! Let's be bold in making the glad Christmas confession, "Jesus Christ is Lord."

A C T I V I T Y

Go through the Christmas cards you have received this year. Select any that are from friends or loved ones who don't know Christ as Savior. Put these cards on the kitchen table, and begin praying for one or two of these people at each meal.

Therefore God also has highly exalted Him and given Him the name which is above every name, that at the name of Jesus every knee should bow, of those in heaven, and of those on earth, and of those under the earth, and that every tongue should confess that Jesus Christ is Lord, to the glory of God the Father.

PHILIPPIANS 2:9–11

Simplifying Service

onfessing the Lordship of Christ also simplifies our service.

We hear a lot these days about cutting back, trimming our schedules, and simplifying our lives. If you want to simplify your life, just ask the two questions Paul asked on the road to Damascus when he met Jesus: "Who are you, Lord?" (Acts 9:5) and "Lord, what do you want me to do?" (v. 6).

Consider also the advice that Mary herself gave to the servants at the wedding in Cana of Galilee. When the wine gave out, Mary said to the servants concerning her son Jesus, "Whatever He says to you, do it" (John 2:5).

Jesus the Sovereign Lord

Can you see how following Jesus simplifies your service? You simply say, "Lord what do You want me to do?" Then do whatever He tells you.

A young preacher was called to a church known for its divisions. One of the women in the church came to him and said, "You're going to have a very difficult job here, trying to please several hundred of us." The preacher said, "I shall not be trying to please several hundred of you. I shall be trying to please one Person only. If I please my Lord, that ought to be good enough for you."

That young preacher gave a wise answer. It doesn't matter whom we displease so long as we please the Lord. And if we displease the Lord, it doesn't matter how many others we please.

Philippians 2:9–11 reminds us that someday every knee shall bow before Jesus Christ and confess Him as Lord. For many, however, it will be too late. This Christmas we need to go boldly to those who have not yet bowed their knee to Jesus and tell them the greatest news anyone could ever hear: "For there is born to you this day in the city of David a Savior, who is Christ the Lord" (Luke 2:11).

A C T I V I T Y

I have already encouraged your family to make a list of people who need to know Christ and to pray for opportunities to witness to them. Review your list together today. Has God been answering prayer? Praise Him! Are there still people who need your witness? Keep praying!

O come, let us worship and bow down: let us

kneel before the Lord our maker.

PSALM 95:6

Where is He that is born King of the Jews?

for we have seen His star in the east,

and are come to worship Him.

MATTHEW 2:2

O Come, Let Us Adore Him, Christ the Lord

he long-awaited day is here. For weeks we have all been preparing for this great day of celebration. The Christmas programs are over. The cookies are baked. The tree is trimmed. The shopping is done. And the gifts are ready, just waiting to be given—and gotten.

I am sure that in the last few days you checked your Christmas list many times so that you didn't miss anyone. Double-checked it to make sure you had bought each and every present for those on your list. And now it is over. If you missed someone or were not able to get that one special gift, now it's too late.

So tell me, did you get anything for Jesus this year? Was He on your Christmas list? You know it is His birthday we are celebrating. What could we give Him?

We all seem to struggle with this at Christmas and end up overlooking Jesus on the very day we celebrate His coming. We get busy at church or in the kitchen or under the tree, and we fail to consider our Lord and Savior. We don't mean to or choose to or want to. But we get so busy with the celebration itself that we sometimes forget whom we are celebrating.

This year what can we give Jesus? What would He want?

A GIFT FOR HIM: READ MATTHEW 2:1-12

This wonderful account recorded by Matthew helps us understand exactly what Jesus wants for Christmas. What is it that the wise men gave Him? Many would say frankincense, myrrh, and gold. But look carefully. Why is it they came? That's right, it was to *worship* the King of the Jews.

That's what our Lord wants from us this Christmas—our worship. The Magi traveled all those miles to see, not a child, but a King. And their response was to worship Him. They understood the truth of the Christmas hymn, "Though an infant now we view him, / he will share his Father's throne, / gather all the nations to him; / every knee shall then bow down. / Come and worship, come and worship, / worship Christ, the newborn King."

This Christmas our great Lord and Savior wants our worship—that's all. Just like the wise men knelt before Him so long ago, we need to come today and bow before Him. The three gifts the Magi brought help us understand exactly who it is we worship this Christmas.

WE WORSHIP THE SON OF GOD: READ JOHN 1:1-3

The little child the Magi worshiped and the Jesus we worship today is not just another man who walked on this earth 2,000 years ago. He is the incarnate Son of God, the One who created us and everything we see and smell and touch. He is very God of very God.

Jesus the Sovereign Lord

The Magi's gift of frankincense to the young child Jesus pointed to Him as the Son of God. This costly, fragrant perfume was used only on the most special of occasions and for worship. Throughout Scripture the burning of incense represents the offering up of prayers and praise to Almighty God. So the Magi's gift demonstrated that Jesus was worthy of worship because of who He was—the Son of God.

Today we must stop and reflect on all that means to us. Because of the marvelous truth that ". . . in him dwelleth all the fulness of the Godhead bodily" (Col. 2:9), those who know Him as Lord and Savior have a sure salvation, power over sin, a glorious message, and much, much more. I believe Michael Card said it well when he wrote these lyrics, "Immanuel, our God is with us. And if God is with us who can stand against us? Our God is with us, Immanuel." This is the One we worship today—Jesus, Immanuel, the Son of God.

WE WORSHIP THE SON OF MAN: READ ISAIAH 53:4-5

It is true that when the Magi came to Bethlehem, they bowed before the very Son of God. But just as true is that they came and bowed before a child who would one day become a man. And this Jesus, the Son of Man, was beaten and punished, suffered and eventually died on the cross for our sins.

The gift of myrrh brought by the Magi to the young Jesus demonstrated His humanity. Myrrh is a bitter spice used in Jesus' day to prepare a body for burial. Their gift of myrrh looked forward to the day the Son of Man would suffer and die as a man for your sins and mine.

On this Christmas Day, as we celebrate the birth of Jesus as a baby, we must never forget what He suffered as the Son of Man on our behalf, the pain and sorrow He went through to provide for us so great a salvation. If it were not for the Son of Man, we would never know salvation, because "...without shedding of blood is no remis-

Jesus the Sovereign Lord

sion" (Heb. 9:22). So today let us worship Him as the Son of Man who purchased our redemption through His suffering and death.

❧ WE WORSHIP THE KING OF KINGS: READ PHILIPPIANS 2:5-11

There is no doubt that the baby whose birth we celebrate was no ordinary child. He came as the Son of God and Son of Man, but there is more. The words from *What Child Is This?* say it so well. "So bring him incense, gold and myrrh; / come peasant, king to own him. / The King of kings salvation brings; / let loving hearts enthrone him." He is the King of Kings.

It is clear that when the Magi came to Jerusalem they were seeking a king. Their gift of gold, the most precious of metals, indicated that they understood the one they would find was royalty. But what they may not have realized is that the child-king they bowed before was none other than the King of all kings.

This Christmas as we celebrate Jesus' virgin birth, His sinless life, His sacrificial death, and His triumphant resurrection, may we keep in mind that one day He will return as King of Kings. On that day ". . . every knee shall bow, of things in heaven, and things in earth, and things under the earth" (Philippians 2:10). And we will reign with Him forevermore.

This year let us remember to give Jesus a very special gift. Let us worship before Him today as the Son of God, the Son of Man, and the King of Kings. It is the only thing He wants. And it is a gift He richly deserves!

A C T I V I T Y

Have everyone in the family make a list of at least five things they have because Jesus came to earth, died for our sins, rose again, and reigns in heaven. Then gather around the Christmas tree and sing "He Is Lord!" Conclude this time by thanking God for what He has done for you through Jesus Christ.

Jesus the Satisfying Life

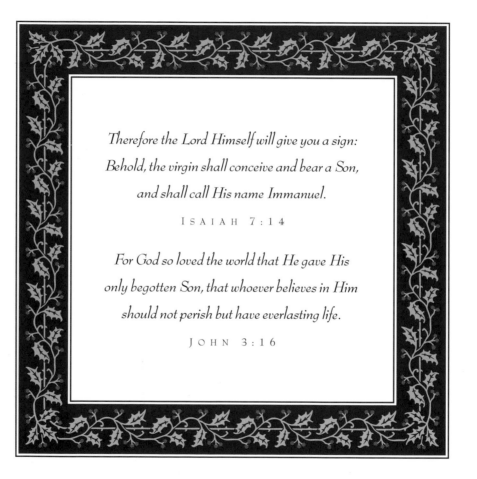

Therefore the Lord Himself will give you a sign:
Behold, the virgin shall conceive and bear a Son,
and shall call His name Immanuel.

ISAIAH 7:14

For God so loved the world that He gave His
only begotten Son, that whoever believes in Him
should not perish but have everlasting life.

JOHN 3:16

Eternal Life

esus did not come into this world at Christmastime to make us nice people. He came to make us new creatures. He was born of a virgin so that we might be born again. He became the Son of Man so that we might become the sons and daughters of God. Our Lord came to earth in order for us to go to heaven. The Savior laid down His life to give us eternal life.

The birth of Jesus is a foundation stone of this world's redemption. It is not incidental but fundamental to our faith. Without the virgin birth, our faith would collapse like the proverbial house built on the sand.

We must remember that God cannot merely overlook our sin and call it mercy. If He did so, He would cease to be a holy God. God's holiness demands that all *sin* must be punished. If a judge knowingly acquits a guilty man, the judge himself is condemned. God's holiness demands that there must be a full payment for sin.

This full payment was made by the substitutionary death of the virgin born Son of God. He had to be a man in order to die for our sins, but He had to be sinless in order to pay the sin debt. By means of both the cradle and the cross, God is now just and the justifier of those who believe in Jesus.

Remember:

He came as He did—virgin-born—

To be what He was—the God-man.

He was what He was, to do what He did—die as a substitute.

He did what He did, to change what we were—lost sinners.

He changed what we were, to make us what we are—new creatures.

A C T I V I T Y

Let family members share their own salvation experience. Pray for others in your immediate and extended family who do not have a clear testimony of having received Jesus Christ as their personal Savior and Lord.

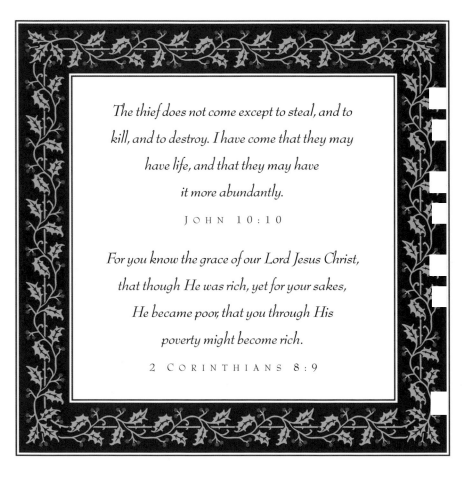

The thief does not come except to steal, and to kill, and to destroy. I have come that they may have life, and that they may have it more abundantly.

JOHN 10:10

For you know the grace of our Lord Jesus Christ, that though He was rich, yet for your sakes, He became poor, that you through His poverty might become rich.

2 CORINTHIANS 8:9

Enriched Life

·⟶🦋

 esus came that we might have *abundant life*. There is a vast difference between mere existence and abundant life. Every soul made in the image of God will exist forever. The human personality could no more cease to exist than God Himself could cease to exist.

There was a time when you did not exist. There never will be a time, however, when you will cease to be. The human personality will go on—endless, timeless, dateless through all eternity.

While we have existence with our first (physical) birth, we have abundant life through our second (spiritual) birth.

It is this abundant life that we all desperately need. There are some who think they want to live forever who do not even know what to do on a rainy afternoon. Jesus came not necessarily to add years to our life, but to add life to our years.

Some college students were asked to define life for the school paper. Here are some definitions that won honorable mention:

"Life is a jail sentence that we get for the crime of being born."

"Life is a disease for which the only cure is death."

"Life is a joke that isn't even funny."

These young people were privileged enough to be in college, and supposedly they have fine minds. Nonetheless, they have gotten it backward.

The Scripture teaches that Jesus Christ became poor that we might become rich. Our dear Savior left the splendors of heaven and was born into deep poverty. Heaven's King was born in a barn—a Monarch in a manger.

When He came into Jerusalem in what is known as His triumphant entry, He came riding on a borrowed donkey; and when He was buried, He was laid away in a borrowed tomb.

Yet it is through His poverty that we have this abundant life. Christmas means a life abundantly rich.

We are not talking about the gospel of cash and Cadillacs with the key to Fort Knox. We are talking about true riches.

We are sons and daughters of God. We are kings and priests unto God. We possess all things that pertain to life and godliness.

To understand how rich Christmas has made you, add up everything you have in Christ that money cannot buy and death cannot take away.

A C T I V I T Y

Ask the members of the family to take inventory of their true riches and to give thanks for all that God has provided. Make a list of the riches that you have in Christ—things that money cannot buy.

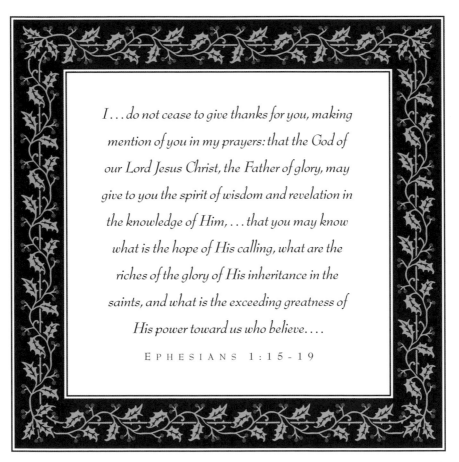

I . . . do not cease to give thanks for you, making mention of you in my prayers: that the God of our Lord Jesus Christ, the Father of glory, may give to you the spirit of wisdom and revelation in the knowledge of Him, . . . that you may know what is the hope of His calling, what are the riches of the glory of His inheritance in the saints, and what is the exceeding greatness of His power toward us who believe. . . .

EPHESIANS 1:15-19

Empowered Life

he power locked up in an atomic particle waiting to be released through nuclear fission is incredible. When the atom is split, it releases power in a ratio of one to six million.

This power is insignificant, however, when compared to the power wrapped up in a seemingly helpless baby lying on the straw in a cattle barn. Jesus came to earth that first Christmas to cause a release of spiritual energy that would shake universes.

Paul wanted the saints at Ephesus to open their spiritual eyes to this power that was inherently theirs through the birth, death, resurrection, and ascension of the Savior. The abundant life that Jesus offers brings with it abundant power.

God made the first Adam and gave to him incredible power and authority (Gen. 1:26). Adam was to have dominion over all the earth. He was to be king of the earth.

The tragedy is that the first Adam "blew it." He gave his power and authority over to Satan. No doubt about it—Satan was a con artist who deceived Adam. Nonetheless, faithless and disobedient Adam yielded his authority to Satan and became Satan's slave. The authority that God had graciously given to the human race was now legally lost.

Here is the reason God was born a man at Christmas. Dominion was graciously given, and then legally lost. Now it must be righteously regained.

The authority was given at first to a man. It was lost by a man. It had to be regained by a Man.

Jesus became a man and took flesh and blood so "that through death He could destroy him that had the power of death" (Heb. 2:14). Satan is now a defeated foe. God did not defeat him as God but rather defeated him as Holy Man. That Man is the Christ of Christmas. Dominion was legally lost by a man; it has been righteously regained by the God-Man.

Now through the miracle of abundant life that same incredible power that Jesus displayed when He arose triumphant from the grave has been graciously given to a new race of creatures—the twice-born.

A C T I V I T Y

Discuss demonstrations of earthly power that you have seen or know about. Then search the newspapers for illustrations of satanic power. Next, rejoice in the abundant power we have that overcomes Satan because of the birth of Bethlehem's Babe.

And she brought forth her firstborn Son, and

wrapped Him in swaddling cloths, and laid Him

in a manger, because there was no room

for them in the inn.

LUKE 2:7

Ennobled Life

ith Christmas past, many are trying to recover from days of rush, frustration, indigestion, and industrial-strength irritation.

Jesus seems to be forgotten and left standing behind the door. No wonder a little girl was heard to pray, "Forgive us our Christmases."

If the world has little room for Jesus even on Christmas, what about the rest of the year? That incident in Bethlehem foreshadowed the lifetime rejection that heaven's King would receive.

Not only was He born in a stable, but He was crucified outside the city walls between two thieves and buried in a borrowed tomb. Indeed, He was despised and rejected by men (Isa. 53:3).

What caused this blunder at Bethlehem so long ago?

Could it have been ignorance? With a more receptive heart the innkeeper might have known. Mary and Joseph knew. The shepherds and the wise men knew. God reveals Himself to those who really want to know.

Could it have been indifference? Mary was "great with child." Couldn't the innkeeper have given his own room to her?

Could it have been involvement? Maybe the innkeeper was just too busy making money. The inn was filled with guests, and his pockets were filled with money. The spirit of King Midas may have caused him to miss heaven's King. I wonder if it might have been different if Mary and Joseph had held up a purse of gold!

Ignorance, indifference, involvement—these are still the Christmas killers. Yet the Christ of Christmas brings ennobling life to those who still seek Him.

If you want to find Him, don't ask the crowd where He is. You will find Him where you will always find Him—despised and rejected of men. He will be on the outside of the stable, not on the inside with the crowd.

"Therefore Jesus also, that He might sanctify the people with His own blood, suffered outside the gate. Therefore let us go forth to Him outside the camp, bearing His reproach. For here we have no continuing city, but we seek the one to come" (Heb. 13:12–14).

When you find Him, you will discover the enduring glory of Christmas. His presence will transform the barn into a palace, and the manger will become a throne.

A C T I V I T Y

Divide today's newspaper among family members and see how the Christmas season has room for everything but Jesus. Let the family members consider what it means to bear His shame and share His glory.

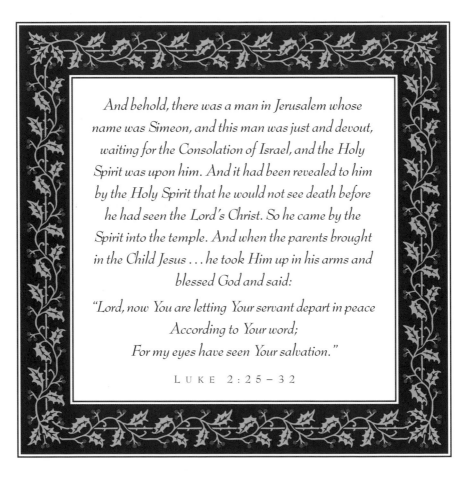

And behold, there was a man in Jerusalem whose name was Simeon, and this man was just and devout, waiting for the Consolation of Israel, and the Holy Spirit was upon him. And it had been revealed to him by the Holy Spirit that he would not see death before he had seen the Lord's Christ. So he came by the Spirit into the temple. And when the parents brought in the Child Jesus . . . he took Him up in his arms and blessed God and said:

"Lord, now You are letting Your servant depart in peace According to Your word; For my eyes have seen Your salvation."

LUKE 2:25–32

Expectant Life

irthdays are a time of celebration. Yet if it were not for the birthday of our King, what would every other birthday mean? It could only mean that we are one year nearer death and judgment. Because of Christmas, we can live the abundant life of anticipation and expectation.

Today's Scripture tells of Simeon, a name that means "listening one." Simeon was anticipating the first coming of Jesus. The Christ of Christmas is coming again. As Simeon prepared for His first coming, we should prepare for His glorious second coming. Many devout men of God believe that Christ again is at the door.

Jesus the Satisfying Life

Joseph and Mary brought the baby Jesus to the temple. Simeon took that little baby in his arms, held Him close to his heart and declared, "Now I am ready to die. I am completely satisfied. My heart is at rest."

Simeon proclaimed some things about Jesus that need to be proclaimed clearly today.

He is the Christ of deliverance. "My eyes have seen your salvation." No one really is ready for Christmas, much less His second coming, unless they have received this glorious salvation.

He is the Christ of delight. He is "a light to bring revelation to the Gentiles." There is now no need to stumble in darkness when we can walk in the glorious light of Christmas.

He is the Christ of derision. Christ is "a sign which will be spoken against." Not all will love Jesus. He is called mad, devil-possessed, a winebibber and glutton, a blasphemer. If the Gospel is not spoken against, it is not the Bible Gospel that is being presented.

He is the Christ of division. "A sword will pierce through your own soul also." Jesus sends a sword that divides. "Do not think I came to bring peace on earth. I did not to come to bring peace, but a sword" (Matt. 10:34). He brings a new nature that conflicts with our old natures.

He is the Christ of destiny. "This child is destined for the fall and rising of many." Jesus is a stone of stumbling or a sure foundation upon which we build.

In the Christ who came, we are ready for the Christ who is coming again. We have expectant life.

A C T I V I T Y

Let family members tell the dates of their personal birthdays, and then testify of their spiritual birthday. Let the children light a candle and sing Happy Birthday to Jesus.

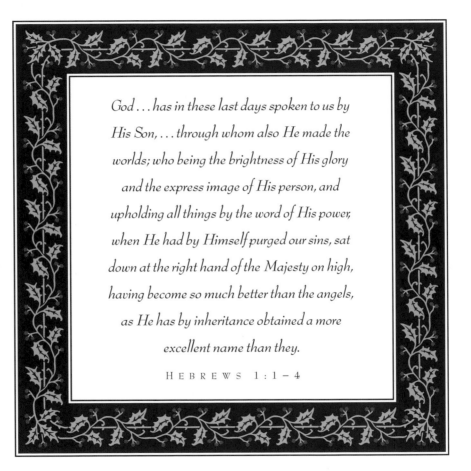

God . . . has in these last days spoken to us by His Son, . . . through whom also He made the worlds; who being the brightness of His glory and the express image of His person, and upholding all things by the word of His power, when He had by Himself purged our sins, sat down at the right hand of the Majesty on high, having become so much better than the angels, as He has by inheritance obtained a more excellent name than they.

HEBREWS 1:1–4

Impassioned Life

The life that Jesus gives is not dull nor common. It is vibrant and impassioned life. That life should be lived with a passionate, emotional, blazing love for the Lord Jesus Christ. His name towers above all others.

H. G. Wells once listed the ten greatest men of history; Jesus Christ was number one on the list. Yet He has no business in a list like that. He is more than a man. We may speak of Charlemagne the Great, Peter the Great, or Alexander the Great. But Jesus is the One and Only. There is no one like Jesus Christ.

It is the uniqueness of Jesus that sets the Christ of Christmas apart from all others. Buddha, Confucius and Mohammed were all leaders, but one can follow their religion without knowing them personally. This is not so with Christ. To take Christ from Christianity would be like taking water from a well, notes from music, and numbers from mathematics.

The key phrase in the book of Hebrews uses the word *better*. It is used thirteen times. God is saying that we can come to know Jesus better, but we can never find anything better than knowing Jesus. He is indeed the superlative Savior. Let's think about His name.

There is wisdom in that name. "God … has … spoken unto us by His Son." This is the earthshaking declaration that God said His last word to humanity—and that word is Jesus Christ. God is love, and love cannot be silent. God has spoken through nature, conscience, history, law, and the prophets. Jesus stood in the wings of history waiting for His time. He cast a long shadow throughout the Old Testament. All of the books of the Old Testament, like tributaries in a mighty river, merge into the last word of God to man—Jesus.

There is wonder in that name. Jesus is the wonderful reason of creation. "He made the worlds." The Baby in Matthew 1 was the Creator of Genesis 1. It is all by Him, for Him, and it is coming to Him.

Jesus is the wonderful regent of creation, "upholding all things by the word of His power." To uphold means to bear a load. Jesus is the glue of the galaxies. Without Him, the cosmos would become a chaos.

Jesus is the wonderful redeemer of creation. "He had by Himself purged our sins." We will be saved by Him alone, or we will not be saved at all. There is no other Savior.

There is worship in that name. Jesus deserves our impassioned worship because of His superior name. "He has by inheritance obtained a more excellent name" than even the angels. We know the names of some of the angels. Michael means "who is like God." Gabriel means "man of God." These angels were mighty and glorious, but Jesus has a more excellent name than they. He is not a messenger of God like Gabriel, but the Word of God Himself.

We worship Him because He is God. He is God upon the throne. Some tell us that we need to "make Him Lord." We are too late for that. He already is Lord. A billion years from now He will still be God upon the throne.

All hail the pow'r of Jesus' name!

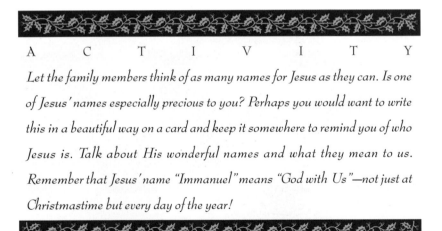

A   C   T   I   V   I   T   Y

Let the family members think of as many names for Jesus as they can. Is one of Jesus' names especially precious to you? Perhaps you would want to write this in a beautiful way on a card and keep it somewhere to remind you of who Jesus is. Talk about His wonderful names and what they mean to us. Remember that Jesus' name "Immanuel" means "God with Us"—not just at Christmastime but every day of the year!